What is the Same?

Written by Catherine Baker

What is the Same?

They all have food. Yum!

We need lots of good food.
This food is good for us!

What is the Same?

They all have pets.

Look at all the pets!
Pets are lots of fun.

What is the Same?

They all have wings.
The wings are not the same.

Look! Things with wings
can go up and up!

What is the Same?

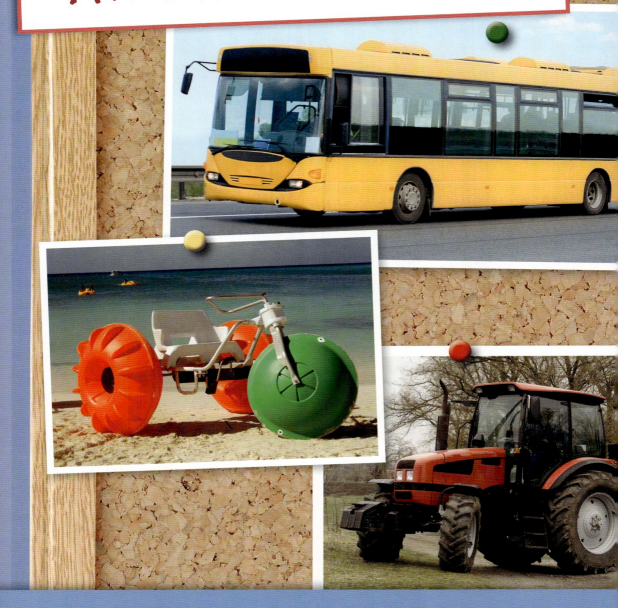

They all have wheels.

Are the wheels the same?

What is the Same?

They all have coats.

Can you see the dog with the cool coat?

Index